CHILDREN EVERYWHERE

Dimensions of Childhood in Early 19th Century New England

Jack Larkin

THE PRESENCE OF CHILDREN

Children in early 19th-century New England were everywhere. In 1800, Timothy Dwight noted that the town of Marblehead "abounds in children," and he set himself to taking an informal census as he passed through: "Several times we stopped our carriage to observe and count them. At one door we numbered eleven, differing very little in their stature, and at every door found a new flock."[1] Dwight thought that the families of Marblehead were exceptionally large, even by the standards of his time; but a 20th-century observer passing through any country town of the period would have shared his wonderment. What demographers call the "age structure" of early nineteenth-century American society was very different from our own, due to its high birth rates. Relative to young adults, the middle-aged, or the elderly, children were far more numerous than they are today. The average age of New England's population in 1830 was 19; today it is 32.[2]

Families were not only larger in size, but child-rearing extended far longer over time. Studies of household structure in the towns of Shrewsbury and Sturbridge, Massachusetts have revealed that parents who were in their mid or late 20's when their first child was born might well not finish launching their children into life until their late 50's or early 60's.[3] During the early 19th century, however, changes were underway which eventually would end the numerical preponderance of children in the New England landscape.

Although their families would still be very large by our standards (averaging 5 or 6 children) young couples in rural New England were deciding to have fewer children than their parents or grandparents had in the 18th century. They accomplished this by shortening the family cycle at both ends. Young women married later every decade, increasingly "skipping" the most fertile years of their reproductive lives. Even more significantly, couples, once married, were making apparently conscious decisions to stop having children earlier; women married in the 1820s and 30s had their last child 3 or 4 years earlier than those married in the 1780s and 90s. This was a response to a changing social and economic environment. Agriculture lost its grip on New England's economy; in the new world of artisanal, commercial and industrial enterprise prospective parents came to look differently at the costs and benefits of child rearing. Most importantly, parents seem to have become increasingly concerned with not having any more children than they could expect to help establish firmly in life.[4]

A family scene used as the frontispiece sets the stage for a family-oriented book. Jacob Abbott, **Fireside Piety or the Duties and Enjoyment of Family Religion** *(New York, 1834).*

CONTINUITY, CONTRAST AND CHANGE

The beginning of conscious family limitation, happening first in New England, was part of a long-term movement toward our own world of childhood — a world of small families and low childhood mortality, Sesame Street and supermarkets, school systems and family-service bureaucracies, peer pressure and organized sports, the "serial monogamy" of divorce and remarriage. This is an interpretive essay about some, but far from all, of the dimensions of childhood in the early nineteenth century. It tries to relate the life of children to the institutions and activities of the New England community, looking both at how things were changing and at instructive contrasts with our own time.

As commercial and industrial villages emerged out of the countryside after 1790 to become distinctively different places to live and work, life in rural New England became more complicated and more diverse for both children and adults. An ever-increasing proportion of men — artisans, merchants, and professionals — practiced full-time trades other than farming. Although the material standard of living rose for most, wealth was becoming more unequally distributed. Religious diversity came with the rapid growth of denominations. By the 1830s even within a single New England town some dimensions of childhood — work, play, schooling, discipline — could vary considerably. Others — patterns of illness and mortality, everyday care and rearing — were elements of continuity, both across the community and with the seventeenth- and eighteenth-century past.

The "arrival of new baby" seems to be as much of a surprise for this young girl as it was for three-year-old Susan Blunt of Merrimack, New Hampshire. Rhymes for the Nursery, Mother Goose's Pocket of Pleasures *(Boston, 1875), p. 72.*

BEARING AND CARING FOR CHILDREN

A child's entry into the world was an uncertain venture which could end in disaster for both mother and baby. With many pregnancies ending with the mother's death, and many more with serious complications, it is no wonder that even the most devoted mothers were known to dread the ordeal of childbirth.[5] Yet despite its difficulties and dangers, birth took place at home in the context of familiar people and surroundings. An older pattern centered around the midwife and the assistance of female kin and neighbors. Childbirth, like child-rearing, had traditionally been a woman's preserve. But beginning in the later 18th century, male physicians were successfully challenging the older practices. Confident of their superior training and determined to make "obstetrics" a medical specialty, they had become dominant in the upper and middle levels of urban society. By the first decade of the 19th century, most rural physicians were also delivering babies. In country towns, physician-assisted childbirth was most common in center villages among the more prosperous, while the poor, the more isolated, and those suspicious of orthodox medicine tended to remain with midwifery.[6]

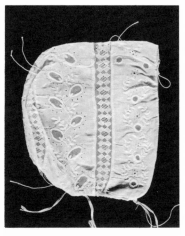

Hand-embroidered white mull cap for an infant, with thread lace bands and insertions. The cap was fitted by pulling up or releasing the drawstrings encased in each side of the embroidered strips and tied with a woven tape string. c. 1835-40. (OSV Collections 26.55.127B).

A recent or an imminent birth was often an occasion for a sister's or mother's visit. Young children were sometimes sent away to keep them out from under foot, but perhaps more frequently they remained at home. Susan Blunt of Merrimac, New Hampshire described her own first encounter, at age three, with her new-born brother:

> Not long after this she [Susan's mother] was not at the breakfast table, and I went to find her. She was in bed in the spare room, and

Maternal Affection. **The American Juvenile Keepsake for 1836**, *Mrs. Hofland, ed. (New York, 1836), pp. 10-11.*

a strange woman sat by the fire with a little baby in her arms. I walked up to her and took hold of its head with both hands. Mother spoke from the bed and said "You must be very careful and not hurt your little brother."

Susan's evident surprise also suggests that the knowledge of a pregnancy was often not shared with children. The dress styles of the period could easily have concealed it, and there seem to have been strong inhibitions against the discussion of such "indelicate" subjects.

Left: Child's night chair with boot jack sides and geometric floral design. Height of back: 18¹/₂". (OSV Collections 5.43.7). Right: Child's fancy night chair with four-spindle back and gilt stencilling on crest rail. Height of back: 20³/₈". (OSV Collections 5.43.5).

Most commonly, mothers nursed their infants. If the mother died, became severely ill or lost her milk supply, it was possible to "bring a child up by hand" with cow's milk, broth, and "pap." The urgency with which both medical and domestic advice writers recommended nursing suggests that there were at least some mothers who consciously chose not to nurse. However, in the absence of much direct evidence, it is very difficult to determine who they were, or how many. Aristocratic English mothers had been frequently criticized for their reluctance to nurse their own children, and it may be that writers feared that well-to-do American women would follow their example.[8]

Toilet training, openly discussed today, was also apparently considered too indelicate for anything but a very occasional medical reference. A Philadelphia physician, writing in 1826 advocated that training begin at one month![9] But in view of the enormous amount of work that went into keeping clothes clean, it seems reasonable to suppose that there was a strong practical impetus in the direction of training children early. Since the early nineteenth century was marked by an increasing concern for domestic order and cleanliness, this may have been even more important for mothers of the time than for their predecessors.

The veil on the woman's hat indicates that she is mourning the infant in the cradle in this illustration for a dialogue about life and death between a mother and her son. The Reverend T. H. Gallaudet, **The Child's Book on the Soul** *(5th ed.: Hartford, 1841), pp. 32-33.*

Babies were ordinarily weaned around the age of one year. Medical writers suggested that the process be a gradual one, but their advice was not always followed; young John Davis Long of Buckland, Maine, was weaned quite abruptly by separating him completely from his mother for four days.[10]

Often infants slept in cradles or cribs, but many, it is clear, slept right in their parents' beds. New Englanders of the early nineteenth century and earlier were substantially more casual than later generations have come to be about certain kinds of physical privacy. Children most commonly slept two or three to a bed or shared a bed with an adult — grandmother, aunt, "help," or lodger — and adults of the same sex frequently slept together as well.[11] Edward Jenner Carpenter, of Greenfield, Massachusetts, for instance, was so firmly molded by his childhood sleeping habits that as an apprentice lodging on his own he would make special efforts "to find somebody to sleep with" if his regular roommate was gone.[12]

From the moment of birth, children's lives were precarious. They died in far greater numbers than they do today, and whenever children fell ill their parents were anxiously aware of the very real dangers involved. Before the antibiotics and immunizations of the 20th century, infectious disease took the greatest toll of life for all but the very old. Children were the most vulnerable to infection. Although the viral "childhood diseases" such as measles, mumps and chicken pox were not ordinarily fatal, they were more dangerous than they are today because they left children vulnerable to other infections. The major killers of children were the diseases we now know as scarlet fever, whooping cough, diphtheria, typhoid, typhus and cholera.[13]

The first year of life was by far the riskiest; one of every seven infants did not survive that long. Often dying in the first few days after birth, they succumbed to a wide variety of infections of the stomach and chest, the effects of premature birth, trauma from difficult deliveries, and birth defects, many of which today would be correctable.[14]

If they survived infancy, New England children had about one chance in ten of dying before adulthood. Even with childhood death rates some ten times as high as our own, life expectancy in rural New England was as good as that of any place in the world in the early 19th century, and much better than in most. New England cities, because of

Busy streets were dangerous places for children like this news-
boy dashing in front of the horse drawn wagon to sell his papers.
S. W. Landers, Spectacles for Young Eyes, Boston
(Boston, 1863), pp. 22-3.

their comparatively high population density and poor sanitation, were considerably less healthy places.[15]

In this disease environment, the death of at least one child in a family was an expectable occurrence. What is now a rare and disastrous stroke of fate was the experience of most families. But the greater frequency of death in childhood does not seem to have made the experience less emotionally shattering for parents. Lucy Buffum Lovell's anguished remembrance registers both how parents felt and how dreaded infections were passed along within families and communities:

> Two days after Caroline was taken from us, Edward became ill. I cannot again bear to tell the story of suffering which came to this last of our children. Our despair was utter when the physicians told us that he was afflicted with scarlet fever, the disease which they decided had taken Caroline. Sister Elizabeth Chaces's little boy, John Gould, who attended Caroline's funeral, had been seized with the same illness on his return home, and lived only about two days, suffering beyond description. He had died Wednesday. A little girl in our own neighborhood also had died after a short sickness of forty-eight hours. We felt horribly hopeless and desperate.[16]

Edward Lovell died within three days; his parents lost three children in less than two years. The grim logic of infection meant that some families would be devastated by multiple deaths from the same disease, like that of the New Hampshire doctor who told Susan Blunt's mother that "he had buried seven little children, all that he ever had."[17] Those families who escaped childhood mortality entirely could count themselves fortunate.

Although less dramatic, mortality in adulthood was likewise higher than it is today, and it too had a significant impact on children. Death in childbirth for women, from work accidents for men, and from consumption (tuberculosis) and other diseases struck many in the prime of life. Because of these hazards, and because parents were considerably older when their last child was born, children were much more likely to experience the death of parents while they were still young and dependent. Childhood reminiscences of the period speak frequently of two themes of dis-

Colored lithograph, (12¹/₂ x 8¹/₂), part of a series of mourning pictures published by J. Baillie. The framed example in the OSV collections memorializes a young man of 18 who died of yellow fever in New Orleans on September 4, 1847.
(OSV Collections 20.8.30).

location: the uprooting and economic vulnerability of a family without a father and provider, and the emotional wrenching of a mother's death, often coupled with adjustment to a stepmother.[18]

The family record of Isaac and Polly Watson Dow notes the deaths of three of the four oldest children in March and April 1831. One of the boys, Daniel, died on his brother Stilman's eighth birthday. Two more children were born later, one of whom grew to adulthood. The three-stanza poem describes the children who died. The record is handwritten in ink on paper, which has been glued to a spruce bark panel and varnished. The split banister frame is ebonized and gilded.
(OSV Collections 20.21.22).

Even more important to the texture of life than these milestones and crises was the daily care of children. Like children everywhere, those in New England households had to be fed, washed, dressed and watched. The kitchen, with its open fireplace and heavy pots at child height, was a particularly dangerous place; scalding and burning were real dangers. Particularly in center villages, the road outside the house could likewise be dangerous, with heavy wagon and horse traffic and no safety arrangements. For the first child or two to arrive, mothers had complete responsibility; increasingly as the family grew, older children took

on some of the burden. The youngest children in large families probably spent more time under the direct care of an older sister or even a "hired girl" than of their mother. This diffusion of responsibility was largely due to the size of early 19th-century families and the sheer amount of work involved in maintaining a household. In families where women's roles and workloads were changing and a new "theory" of mothering was being adopted this was decreasing; but there was still likely to be considerably more sharing of child care than is usual today.[19]

Above left: *Handsewn blue, white and brown checked cotton dress for a child. Originally made with a 7¹/₂" hem which was let down to ¹/₃" as the child grew. The right sleeve has a large elbow patch. c. 1810-1825. This garment descended in the Wilber family of Swansea, Massachusetts. (OSV Collections 26.55.13).*
Above right: *Young girl's dress. The factory-printed cotton design has small Greek crosses with dots inside. The dress has short puffed raglan sleeves and vertical gathers on the bodice front and back. The drawstring at the neck is a white silk ribbon. c. 1835-1840. (OSV Collections 26.33.198).*

Children playing under the watchful eye of a hired helper.
Charlotte Elizabeth, **Short Stories** *(New York, n.d.), p. 83.*

WORK

Today the world of work and the world of childhood are radically separated. In rural New England, work had long been seen as virtually continuous with life itself. Two long-traditional aspects of the region's society were responsible: the necessities of an unmechanized rural economy and a widely shared conviction that idleness was a source of moral evil. But by the early 19th century, young children could have experienced work in considerably different ways, depending on their family's residence, household composition, and economic situation.

When John Davis Long of Buckland, Maine, was five years old, his father recorded that he helped to shell corn:

> He has an old box with an iron rod laid lengthwise upon it, which is held in place with an old day book and by seating himself upon it a straddle the iron. He shells fast the ears of corn by holding them with one hand against the sharp edge of the iron, while with the other he turns them first one way, then the other — very sociable all the while.[20]

In the countryside, farm and family were intertwined, almost indistinguishable. The work of the farm encompassed a complete spectrum of necessary tasks, for small and unskilled hands as well as for older and more knowledgeable ones. From the ages of six or seven on, and often beginning earlier in at least a semi-serious way, both girls and boys were significant members of the farm labor force. Each member of the family was an interlocking member of a productive unit directed by the head of the household. Beginning like John Davis with shelling corn or with weeding the garden, children took on increasingly difficult tasks as they grew up. Girls worked with their mothers in learning crucially important sewing, cooking and dairying skills; boys labored with their fathers in barn, fields, and shop.

The pressure of work on children was surely greatest among poorer families. Having spent his early years picking stones, guiding the oxen at the plough, and arising at sunrise to do chores before breakfast, Horace Greeley remembered that:

> Being the older son of a poor and hard-working farmer, struggling to pay off the debt he had incurred in buying his farm, and to support his increasing family, I was early made acquainted with labor.[21]

A boy pushing a wheelbarrow loaded too precariously
with cornhusks. Jacob Abbott, **Rollo at Work**
(New York, 1869), p. 22.

In hard-pressed artisans' or widows' families, young boys were often "hired out" to do chores or fieldwork for neighbors and girls to do housework or care for children. The organization of work on the basis of the household, with a prominent place for children's work, persisted in many new forms of early 19th-century economic activity. In the textile manufacturing villages of southern New England, much of the labor force was made up of family groups, with children as young as seven or eight working in the factories along with their older brothers and sisters. Hiram Munger, the son of a poor mechanic, remembered his earliest years of factory work as "American slavery in the *second degree*."[22] Whether in the factory, on a small farm, or in a struggling village household, economically marginal parents sometimes had to exploit themselves and their children in order to survive.

For most children of better-off families, the pressure of work was usually less, although it was almost never absent. Because Yankee culture valued work so highly, even the children of the most prosperous households, where farm laborers and household help could make their work unnecessary, were rarely allowed to be idle. Such conviction could sometimes be pushed to the extreme. Francis Underwood thought that a sizeable minority of rural New England children were driven hard, beyond any economic necessity, and allowed little time for play because of their parents' ingrained aversion to leisure.

In the center villages, and to a greater extent in the cities, the identity of household and workplace, family and workforce, was becoming less complete. An artisan's, professional's or merchant's household, living on a few acres or less of land, was not an integrated productive unit in the same way as one on the farm. The work of a minister, a storekeeper, or a printer, although carried on in or near his home, consisted of tasks with which most of his family could have only a partial involvement. Without the farm's wide spectrum of tasks, young children were less likely to be engaged in directly productive work. The professional man's situation was the most clear-cut; his family could have little direct impact on his sermon, his legal brief, or the treatment of his patients. Artisans' and storekeepers' children might help around shop or store at times, and some boys began early paternal "apprenticeships"; but many sons — probably most — would follow a trade different from their fathers', and the work of both children and their mothers was far less involved to the success of most commercial and artisanal enterprises.[24]

Help was needed with farm chores in any season. Work continued throughout the cold weeks of winter with the gathering of logs for firewood and fencing materials. Jacob Abbott, **The Jonas Stories: Jonas on the Farm in Winter** *(New York, 1855), p. 35.*

Sampler (15¹/₄" x 17") made in Sturbridge on a striped factory-made cotton. With the alphabets stitched twice in upper case, once in lower case letters and, the numerals from 1-10, it is a marking sampler, with choices of letters and numbers used for marking textiles. Black thread is used for the letters and borders. The flowers are yellow with green leaves (OSV Collections 64.1.15).

Homer Merriam's father was one of the few men who operated a farm in the center village of West Brookfield, Massachusetts, and Homer recalled that, "I used to think it hard that I had a task to perform while my mates had none."[25]

In some non-farming families, there was some concern that there was less real work to go around than was good for young children. Lydia Maria Child, the writer of cookery and domestic advice books, who had grown up in a village tradesman's household and married a lawyer, voiced her conviction in 1831 that "it is very important, and very difficult, to furnish young children with sufficient employment."[26] Her discussion of this problem, full of suggestions about tasks that could be given children and skills that could be taught to keep them occupied, was an implicit recognition that in some households the broad and inclusive spectrum of farm tasks had greatly diminished.

Yet although a "middle-class" domestic order was beginning to take shape, work continued to be intertwined with the other activities of a childhood in a way which few contemporary American children have experienced. In center village households, young girls still sewed and embroidered, helped with the housework and sometimes with cooking, and seeded the garden with their brothers. Young boys ran errands, cut and carried wood, and saw to the horse, if the family owned one.[27]

This illustration is taken from the short story, "The Hated Task,"
which tells about young Harriet who was feeling very provoked
because her mother had given her a "long piece of hemming."
Charlotte Elizabeth, Short Stories, *p. 102.*

PLAY

I If the work experiences of early 19th-century children have few counterparts in modern America, play provides a link across the generations. Children are surely culturally closest to their predecessors of 150 years ago when playing. Over a long span of time, one generation of children has passed its games on to the next through oral traditions which have allowed plenty of room for regional, local, and neighborhood variation but have also preserved many things intact. "Buzz" and "Puss in the Corner," to cite two examples, are played by New England children today just as they are described in early 19th-century books — books which they surely never read. The rules of marbles and numerous varieties of tag have likewise changed little over the years. Early 19th-century children

Child's wooden sled decorated with a painted yellow horse. (OSV Collections 77.4.7).

played fantasy games in the kitchen, the bedchamber, the yard or an adjoining pasture; they used themes from Bible stories, recent history, or moralistic children's fiction, rather than from Star Wars or situation comedies, but the form seems to have persisted to the present. Children played house with "rag babies" and "bits of broken china," fought Revolutionary battles and Napoleonic campaigns, or held "prayer meetings and preached sermons."[28] In the summer, boys, although ordinarily not girls, swam and fished. In the fall, they might go on expeditions to pick nuts and berries. In winter, they skated, sledded and coasted. Rolling hoops, playing "the Grace," stickball or roundball would begin as snow cleared and the spring advanced. Rural girls could run, tramp through the woods and play active games with a freedom

Child's wooden sled, with initials WSP, dated 1846. The word, "clipper", appears on each side runner, still legible although the paint is flaking. (OSV Collections 77.4.2).

A group of boys on a town common playing an unidentified game which involves pitching a ball to be hit with a special kind of stick. From Joseph Breck, **The Young Florist or Conversations on the Culture of Flowers and On Natural History** *(Boston, 1833), p. 124.*

A yoke of oxen whittled by hand out of pine. The yoke has an iron ring. Each animal has a tail of twisted rope. They are 7³/₄" from rump to nose, 6" across the backs and 4¹/₂" in height to the top of the yoke (OSV Collections 1.209.77).

10 to 100 families gathered together, had a wider range of playmates. Their play was spontaneous and without adult direction, as is most children's play today; strikingly missing was the 20th century's range of organized children's activities.

Rural children's toys were simple, homemade contrivances; store-bought, shop-made ones were rare. For little girls accustomed to "rag-babies" the arrival of a real doll, "with glass eyes and real hair," was a wonder, to be "laid away very carefully."[29] Today's children may no longer be producers, but they have become toy consumers, participants in a multi-billion-dollar part of our market economy. Children from homes in quite modest circumstances today have toy collections which would have stunned even their wealthiest counterparts in times past.

which their urban counterparts, raised in a more confining environment, did not have. Some center village families may have begun to restrict girls' play as well, but certainly not all of them. Children who lived on farms often had only their brothers and sisters to play with; children in villages, with

Games like jumping rope were encouraged as a "healthy form of exercise which tends to make the form graceful." A favorite then and now it only required a rope and two people willing to turn it. Lydia Maria Child, **The Girl's Own Book** *(Boston, 1833), p. 103.*

SCHOOLING

Contrasting his native New England to the rest of the United States in 1823, Henry Dana Ward of Shrewsbury, Massachusetts, called it "the land of schools."[30] Schooling at some level was part of the lives of almost all children in the region; in greater numbers than elsewhere in their own country or in most of Europe, they learned to read, writer and cipher. Up to the middle of the 18th century, educational opportunities for girls had lagged behind, and even at the time of the Revolution many adult women were illiterate. But by 1820 the efforts of generations of rural schoolmasters in thousands of district schools had resulted in nearly full literacy for both sexes.[31]

In the thought and practice of most rural people, teaching and learning, although important, were not complicated affairs. Contemporary testimony leaves little doubt that early 19th-century children were taught primarily by rote. They memorized and recited the alphabet, the definition and spelling of words, the rules of grammar and the facts of arithmetic, even long prose passages, often long before they understood them.[32]

As much as New Englanders like to think that their free schools guaranteed a rough equality of opportunity, in reality children's educational experiences depended greatly on their parents' status and resources. Center villages concentrated educational advantages as well as settlement. Life there was less directly dependent on the seasonal rhythms of farming, and schools stayed open longer. Village children did not have far to walk, and did not have to be kept home in bad weather. The center village school district was usually the first in any community to regularize textbooks, bring new subjects like United States history and composition into the curriculum, build an improved and enlarged schoolhouse, or hire female teachers for the winter term.[33]

Children whose families had a pressing need for their work attended irregularly. Some might miss whole terms for years at a time. Dire poverty kept others away, like Hiram Munger who "was often dissatisfied with staying at home without clothes to go to school or to meeting but very little. I was nearly 16 years old before I could write, or read a paper; and I could not cipher at all."[34] On the other hand, the children of the well-to-do or the more enterprising families of the middling sort attended school much more consistently. The children of bookbinder Dan Merriam, who wanted "to give them the best advantages he could for education," attended school in West Brookfield center village winter and summer, "while it kept, some six or eight months in the year."[35] Such chil-

School lessons were set to be learned and recited individually to the teacher. The youngest students, the "abcdarians," sat on the front benches to learn their alphabets and phonics. Jacob Abbott, Rollo at School *(Boston, 1839), p. 155.*

dren often looked forward to further instruction in an academy or female seminary, even if only for a term or two.[36]

Even in the center village, however, schooling was a far more haphazard, informal and loosely organized process than it is today. Children did not think of themselves as first-graders, third-graders, or fifth-graders, because the specific age-graded categories and notions of unvarying yearly academic progress familiar to us from our own schooling did not exist. The pupils who crowded together in a district school for the winter term frequently ranged from as young as three years to as old as twenty — as the educational reformer Horace Mann described it, from "infants but just out of their cradles" to "men who had been enrolled . . . in the militia."[37] Teachers were often younger than their oldest pupils. In such an environment, simply maintaining order was a difficult task for many of them. Violent confrontations between schoolmasters and the older "boys" were common enough that many children witnessed them at least once during their school years. A teacher who lost a fist fight or was successfully "barred out" of his school often departed the district precipitately, leaving the school "broken up" before the end of the term. The harsh discipline

reported of many district schoolmasters — "the liberal application of birch and ferule" as Horace Greeley remembered it — was a long-traditional way of providing motivation for learning; for teachers without adequate training or a natural gift for instruction, it may well have seemed the only way of dealing with such a heterogeneous mixture of ages and capacities.[38]

The school records kept by David Goodale, Sr., who taught in Stow, Massachusetts, from 1810 to 1821, show children there usually beginning school at three or four years of age and sometimes at two. These youngest children came to school with their older brothers and sisters, making it clear

Child's cup. Transfer printed pearlware cup made in England c. 1850-60. 2¹/₂". (OSV Collections 51.12.45).

*A classroom with maps and educational aids was one of the rec-
ommendations of the reformers of district school education.
Jacob Abbott,* The Mount Vernon Reader for Middle Classes
(New York, 1837), p. 173.

that district schools served the purposes of child care, as well as instruction. An eight-year-old or even younger child might well have simultaneously played the roles of pupil, learning to read from a primer, and of substitute parent for a younger sibling.[39]

The undifferentiated district school was changing slowly. Many of its characteristics were almost inevitable under conditions of scattered rural settlement and slow transportation. Center village school districts began to adopt more advanced architectural designs, which provided separate rooms and instructors for younger and older pupils. This marked the first step toward age-grading, but it took decades to spread through the villages and much longer to become the rural norm.[40] Mann clearly believed that the age spread of the typical district schools was excessive and by the end of the 1830's, a change in the age composition of the district school was also getting underway. Part of it may have been due to changing views about the needs of very young children.

Writing in 1836, another reformer, William Alcott, urged mothers not to send their children off to school and its uncertain influences too young, arguing that two-, three- and four-year-olds were better off at home under their mothers' care. In some center villages and urban neighborhoods, infant schools began to appear around 1830 to provide instruction for children who were now thought to be too young for district schooling.[41]

By mid-century, these reformist urgings had become a reality. School attendance figures for some central Massachusetts country towns from the 1850 population census show almost no children under age four attending school, and that they were by then more commonly starting school at five. The proportion of pupils over 17 in the district schools had also declined considerably by 1850. In the 1830s and 40s county schools achieved longer terms and more regular attendance, enabling students to finish their schooling earlier.[42]

Going to school on a windy November day, possibly the beginning of the winter term which traditionally began after Thanksgiving. Schoolyards were generally bare areas, not landscaped playgrounds for recess and dinner hours. Merry's Museum. Vol. VIII, No. 5 (November 1844), p. 129.

CONCEPTS AND PRACTICES
OF CHILD-REARING

Along with other changes in the dimensions of childhood came an increasing emphasis on the early years as a special and developmentally crucial stage of life. Historians now generally agree that the Village period did not see the "invention" of childhood in New England. In the 17th and 18th centuries, children were not perceived as "miniature adults" or merely smaller and less skilled versions of their parents; rather adults had a clear sense, although in a much less age-stratified society, of children's immature capacities and need for nurturance. The much-maligned Puritans both loved their children as children *and* feared for their eternal salvation.[43] But one of the insistent themes of the advice literature on child-rearing which was emerging to great popularity in the 1830s was that the care, education and discipline of children needed much more conscious attention from parents than earlier generations had given it. Childhood was coming to be seen as a uniquely malleable time; parents, and particularly mothers, were set the task of permanently guiding and shaping their children's characters. The stakes were high. Many an early 19th-century mother must have read that her children's future welfare — economic, moral and spiritual — hung on her every decision.[44]

Of course, not everyone read advice literature, advice books did not always agree, and it is not easy to be sure how and to what extent advice was translated into practice. Still, there is good evidence that some of the most popular New England advice books emerged out of the lives of real households and were codifications of experience rather than statements of abstract theory. An increasing concern with child-rearing practices was clearly characteristic of many households and formed part of an emerging New England version of "middle-class" culture. The parents more likely to be putting these ideas into practice were prosperous or aspiring artisans, merchants and professionals in cities and center villages. In such households, mothers who were free from the pressures of farm work (or who had lost that central economic role) were able to devote "surplus" time to the more self-conscious raising of children.[45]

In general, across all levels of life and styles of child-rearing, corporal punishment was more common in the early 19th century than now. So too, probably, was formality and emotional restraint between parents and children, in a Yankee culture which was generally constrained and undemonstrative. Childhood reminiscences frequently sound the theme of deep, but rarely expressed, parental feeling. But it is important to

In this illustration for a short story, "The Walk" by Mrs. J. H. Hanaford, the young girl and her mother find that exercise in the open air is more than a healthy form of exercise. Francis C. Woodworth, American Miscellany of Entertaining Knowledge *(Boston, 1852), p. 118.*

34 remember that the range of variation from one household to another — in emotional tone, methods of discipline, intensity of religious concern — was wide, just as it is today. Accounts of childhood in the period present widely differing styles of family government. Some families were openly affectionate and in many more there were at least some moments of play and relaxation between parents and children. The letters of Salem Towne, Jr. to his wife between 1822 and 1832, and Zadoc Long's journal convey both warm concern and physical expressions of affection for their children. Lyman Beecher played boisterously with his children, although he was also a stern disciplinarian. Young Caroline Lovell managed to engage her father, serious Evangelical minister that he was, in a fantasy storekeeping game.[46]

For most families in the countryside, child-rearing was almost surely more a matter of tradition, habitual pattern, and unspoken assumptions than of conscious choices. Compared with the "middle-class" model, "traditional" New England families were both more loosely governed and more harshly, if erratically, disciplined. Compared to a minister's children, say, a farmer's might be less closely watched but more casually "boxed on

the ears" for a transgression. Susan Blunt, a blacksmith's daughter, matter-of-factly recalled a "very severe whipping" at age three. Minerva Mayo of Orange, Massachusetts, "often had to feel the rod of correction" from her mother; her usually indulgent father, when disturbed at haying:

> ". . . caught me by the arm, and
> gave me a toss into the air, and I
> came down on the head of his rake.
> This raised my stuff, and I yelled so
> loud that I was heard near a mile,
> he then took me and carried me, to a
> heap of stone, and laid me down
> upon the ground, and placed a large
> flat stone upon my back, here I laid
> in this position until I became very
> submissive . . ."

Alcott, perhaps melodramatically, claimed that "I know of whole families, whose mental faculties are dull, as the consequence — I believe — of a perpetual boxing and striking of the head . . . I have seen parents and masters strike the heads of their children with pieces of wood . . . a common-sized tailor's press-board . . . the heavy end of a wooden whip-handle . . ."[48] Where some artisans' and farmers' households were seen as severe,

Discipline and family rules might be spelled out by either parent. **The Very Young Lady's Toilet** *(Philadelphia, n.d.), p. 14.*

others were judged lax and indulgent. "Riding in the country," a minister recalled visiting a farmhouse where:

> half a dozen rude and ungovernable
> boys were racing about the room, in
> such an uproar as to prevent the
> possibility of conversation with the
> father, who was sitting by the fire.
> As I, however, endeavored to make
> some remark, the father shouted
> out, 'Stop that noise, boys.' They
> paid no more heed to him than they
> did to the rain. Soon again, in an
> irritated voice, he exclaimed,
> 'Boys, be still, or I will whip you; as
> sure as you are alive I will.' But the
> boys as accustomed to such threats,
> screamed and quarreled without
> intermission. At last the father said
> to me, 'I believe I have got the worst
> boys in town; I never can make
> them mind me.'[49]

The "middle-class" styles of discipline were likely to be built around a much closer regulation of children's lives and a preference for "moral suasion" — the use on non-physical punishments like isolation and confinement, the withdrawal of affection, and the revocation of privileges. In families with a strong Evangelical religious commitment, child-rearing patterns combined both strictness of control and some use of corporal punishment. John Abbott was a Worcester, Massachusetts minister whose lectures to the mothers of his congregation were published as *The Mother at Home* in 1834. One of Abbott's model cases of discipline seems to represent well what many Evangelicals were striving for:

> 'But Mary,' says the mother, 'you
> have disobeyed me, and you must
> be punished.'
>
> Mary continues to cry, but the
> mother seriously and calmly
> punishes her. She inflicts real pain
> — pain that will be remembered.
> She then says, 'Mary, it makes
> mother very unhappy to have to
> punish you, she loves her little
> daughter and wishes to have her a
> good girl.'
>
> She then perhaps leaves her to
> herself for a few minutes. A little
> solitude will deepen the impression
> made.

*A new age of child rearing was coming, but many parents still preferred the tradition of restraint. Jacob Abbott, **The Jonas Stories: Caleb in Town** (New York, 1855), pp. 36-37.*

Lucy Buffum Lovell, a conscientious Evangelical mother, recounted remarkably similar child-rearing practices.[50] Such households — those described by Samuel Underwood as the "ultra-pious" — fostered a deeply serious atmosphere which could sometimes become highly rigid and repressive. Discipline in the most Evangelical of families stressed the importance of "breaking the will" of young children, sternly repressing youthful attempts at self-assertion and making them docile and obedient in the interests of their eternal salvation.

More "moderate" parents in families like the Wards of Shrewsbury, the Townes of Charlton, the Larcoms of Danvers, the Lymans of Northampton, or the Merriams of West Brookfield, saw discipline more as a matter of teaching children to control their wills rather than breaking them, and gave their children somewhat more leeway.[51] Their practice seems to have been closer to the views of Child's more moderate *The Mother's Book* or even to Alcott's *The Young Mother* which condemned corporal punishment and advocated greater freedom for children's activities. What all the "middle-class" styles had in common was a focused, conscious concern with mothering, an emphasis on order, and an insistent moralism.

Jonas has gone fishing and has been successful, while his country friends Jonas and Oliver clear stones from a field with the help of the ox team. Jacob Abbott, **The Jonas Stories: Jonas on the Farm in Winter** *(New York, 1855), p. 35.*

CHILDREN AND RELIGION

What would be a lifetime of churchgoing for many children began with their baptism. Although Baptists restricted the rite to adults, Methodists and Episcopalians baptized all, as did Unitarians and some Universalists.[52] Children in the Congregational tradition, however, were usually baptized as infants only if at least one of their parents was a full-fledged church member, not simply a member of the congregation. In most Congregational churches in the early 19th century, this requirement was not a mere formality, but demanded that the individual give evidence of a transforming conversion experience. Upon one or both parent's conversion and admission to membership, it was not uncommon for all the children in the family to be baptized together. Whether for infants, older children or adults, the baptismal ceremony normally took place in the meetinghouse during the Sabbath service; but under special circumstances, like illness, it could be performed in a private home. Congregational ministers in Sturbridge, for instance, occasionally baptized children in their mother's sickroom.[53]

When parents went to meeting, children usually accompanied them. In good weather, at least, infants and toddlers often attended.[54] Younger children most often sat with their families in their pews, although in some meeting houses older boys were grouped together in the galleries. Young children were occasionally left home by themselves; in Shrewsbury, Massachusetts it led at least once to disaster. In February of 1799, six-year-old Nathan Goddard and his four-year-old brother Artemas accidentally set fire to their house while the rest of the family was at meeting; the parents and older children returned to find the boys luckily escaped, but the house burned to the ground. Such calamities might have discouraged other parents from leaving part of the family behind, although others may have continued to trust their luck.[55] Some families were strictly regular in their weekly attendance; others were considerably laxer; a minority did not attend at all. The same lack of decent clothing that made young Hiram Munger's schooling so irregular also kept him away from meeting. Local women's charitable societies sewed to clothe poor children for Sunday worship.[56]

By the early 19th century, New Englanders had long abandoned belief in the doctrine of infant damnation, but for many parents their children's spiritual state continued to be an object of deep concern. These concerns began to be expressed in new forms of association and organization. Sabbath schools, often far more carefully organized

Infants were usually christened during Sunday worship, so this scene records a special occasion during the weekly routine. From the Chandler, Wright and Mallory Proof Book. (Courtesy, American Antiquarian Society).

42

and age-graded than the district school, were created in many churches to provide for more effective religious instruction. Women of an Evangelical bent in country towns founded maternal associations to support each other in striving for their children's early conversion.[57] However, despite the wide popularity of stories like that of Nathan Dickerman — a spiritually precocious Boston boy who had joined the church before his death at age eight — very few children joined a church before age 13. Youth — the late teens and early 20s — was the time, particularly for girls, when conversions most commonly occurred. And even among the most devout families, many children were not converted until later in adulthood or, particularly males, not at all, a prospect which caused devout parents much concern.[58] Some children, under intense adult pressure, did spend a considerable part of their early lives wrestling with religious anxiety. Horace Mann, for instance, recalled a boyhood darkened by the grim and forceful Calvinistic preaching of Nathanael Emmons, which impelled him to reject orthodox belief; adult Evangelicals, of course, remembered their childhood struggles as necessary although painful parts of their conversion.[59]

Daily family prayer and Bible-reading were probably not as universal as some of New England's literary propagandists would have it, but still widespread. In many households the Bible was still "read in course" daily; that is, read continuously from beginning to end without commentary or explanation. A great deal of it must have been completely incomprehensible to children.[60]

From the child's point of view, religion probably had its greatest impact on daily life in the observance of the Sabbath. New England had a long tradition of rigorous Sabbath observance since it had been an essential point of Puritan religious reform. In many households, the day was kept very strictly. Play was forbidden, toys were put away, and in the intervals between services and sabbath school, children were allowed only to read or listen to the Bible and other religious literature. Even Mrs. Child, who felt that children under five or six might be allowed to play quietly on the Sabbath, believed that older children should devote the day to religious instruction.[61] In more relaxed households, there was surely some quiet play and "secular" reading allowed, but more boisterous forms of Sunday recreation were seen in country towns only among a small minority of the "actively ungodly."

Both private prayer and family prayer were encouraged in devout families. **Religious Experience and Death of Eliza Van Wyck** *(New York, n.d.), p. 5.*

CONCLUSION

Around 1830, a group of ladies entered a New England parlor "unexpectedly, just as the family was seated at the supper-table. A little girl, about four years old, was obliged to be removed, to make room for us."[62] The account of this incident went on to describe the mother's exemplary firmness in disciplining the child for objecting to her displacement; but what is significant for us is that the removal of a hungry child to make way for unexpected adult company was considered perfectly reasonable and unsurprising, as it would surely not in middle-class families today. Reared, loved, nursed through illness, schooled and written about in the early nineteenth century, rural New England's children were firmly subordinated to the interests and needs of adults. They occupied a less central place in the concerns of that time, even as they dominated its population. Family government in America has become considerably less authoritarian over the years. The proportion of society's resources invested in the care, entertainment and education of children has risen while their numbers relative to adults have declined.

The United States has, in the recent past, been called a "child-centered" society. But there are signs that a new refocusing is underway, as the proportion of the elderly mounts, the birth rate continues to decline, and two-career families become increasingly common. The dimensions of childhood are surely changing again.

"Keep Saved the Memory of Your Ancestors." Family Record of Mowry Saben and Almira Wheaton Saben and their children, Warwick, Massachusetts, 1833. Large roses and green leaves are painted over the arch inscribed with the legend. At the bottom is a view of the family farm at Warwick. After burying the first two children who had died of diphtheria, the Sabens returned home to find that two more children had died of the disease. Almira Wheaton was certified as a teacher of theorem painting in 1828 by Lucy Earle at the Mulberry Grove School in Leicester, Massachusetts. (OSV Collections 20.21.12).

Even at Thanksgiving dinner, New England's great festival, a child might not have a seat at table. Charles Goodrich
The Universal Traveller *(Hartford, 1848), pp. 48-9.*

NOTES

1. Timothy Dwight, *Travels in New England and New York,* ed. by Barbara Miller Solomon (4 vols.; Cambridge, 1969) I, p. 332.

2. These figures are based on the federal population censuses for 1830 and 1980.

3. This conclusion is based on a study of household structure in Shrewsbury and Sturbridge, Massachusetts, using the manuscript population schedules of the federal census, 1790-1850 and the published *Vital Records to 1849* for each town.

4. Grey Osterud and John Fulton, "Family Limitation and Age of Marriage: Fertility Decline in Sturbridge, Massachusetts, 1730-1850," *Population Studies* XXX No. 3, pp. 481-494.

5. Grey Osterud, "The New England Family," (Old Sturbridge Village, Museum Education Resource Packet, 1979); Susan I. Lesley, *Recollections of My Mother* (Boston and New York, 1899), pp. 306, 332, quotes two letters of Anne Jean Lyman about the risks of childbirth.

6. See Catherine M. Scholten, "On the Importance of the Obstetrick Art: Changing Customs of Childbirth in America, 1760 to 1825," *William and Mary Quarterly* Series 3, XXXIV, pp. 427-445.

7. Reminiscences of Susan Blunt, 1913 [covering the years 1828-43], Manchester Historical Association, Manchester, New Hampshire, pp. 2-3. The observation about children's consciousness of childbirth is Caroline Sloat's.

8. See, for example, Josiah Spaulding, *The Female's Guide to Health* (Skowhegan, Maine, 1837), pp. 113-119; Hugh Smith (M.D.), *Letters to Married Ladies* (3rd ed.; New York and Boston, 1832), pp. 80-118. Also Lawrence Stone, *Family, Sex and Marriage in England 1500-1800* (New York, 1977).

9. William Alcott, *The Young Mother* (Boston, 1836), pp. 80-81, discusses the difficulties of keeping "diapers" clean; William De Wees, *A Treatise on the Physical and Mental Treatment of Children* (Philadelphia, 1826), p. 105.

10. Medical books concurred in describing this as the normal age; *Journal of Zadoc Long of Buckland, Maine 1800-1872,* ed. by Pierce Long (Caldwell, Idaho, 1943), pp. 148-9, (Nov. 7-11, 1840).

11. David Flaherty, *Privacy in Colonial New England* (New York, 1973), pp. 76-79 has a general account. *The Life of P. T. Barnum, Written by Himself* (New York, 1855), pp. 40-43 is an account of sharing a bed in his childhood in Bethel, Connecticut. Alcott, *The Young Mother,* pp. 257-262 discusses period practices disapprovingly.

12. Diary, Edward Jenner Carpenter, 1844-45, Greenfield, Massachusetts, American Antiquarian Society.

13. See Richard Shryock, *Medicine and Society in America: 1660-1860* (New York, 1959) for an introductory account.

14. Osterud, "New England Family"; Maris A. Vinovskis, "Mortality Rates and Trends in Massachusetts Before 1860," *Journal of Economic History* XXXII (March, 1972), pp. 184-214.

15. Osterud, "New England Family"; Vinovskis, "Mortality Rates and Trends."

16. Lucy Buffum Lovell, "Diary," 1840-44, *Two Quaker Sisters* (New York, 1937), p. 106.

17. Reminiscences of Susan Blunt, pp. 34-35.

18. Homer Merriam, "My Father's History and Family," in "Annals of the Merriam Family," Merriam-Webster Collection, Beinecke Library, Yale University, Microfilm in OSV Research Library; Lucy Larcom, *A New England Girlhood* (Boston, 1889), pp. 136-160; *Autobiography of Lyman Beecher* (Cambridge, MA, 1961), pp. 216-228, 236-8, 264-274; Harry Allen Grant, *A Journey From Utica To Hartford Fifty Years Ago,* (New York, 1899), pp. 4-7.

19. The Reminiscences of Susan Blunt describes such a family.

20. *Journal of Zadoc Long,* p. 158 (April 11, 1844). I am indebted to Caroline Sloat for constructive criticism of this entire section.

21. Horace Greeley, *Recollections of a Busy Life* (New York, 1868), p. 38.

NOTES

22. For examples, see Asa Sheldon, *The Life of Asa Sheldon* (Woburn, Massachusetts, 1869), pp. 10-35; Reminiscences of Susan Blunt, pp. 17, 19-20; William Williams, Account Book, Shrewsbury, Massachusetts 1823-32, Ward Family Papers, American Antiquarian Society, entry "Widow Haven"; for quote, Hiram Munger, *The Life and Religious Experience of Hiram Munger* (Chicopee Falls, Mass., 1856), p. 3.

23. Francis W. Underwood, *Quabbin: The Story of a New England Town* (New York and London, 1893), pp. 187-8.

24. At the same time, many rural New England households were becoming workplaces in their own right as the expanding market economy, reaching out into the country towns, provided work opportunities like "fitting up" shoes, making palm leaf hats and braiding straw for girls and women. Sometimes these activities were linked to the work of other household members, as with girls who would stitch shoe uppers for their fathers and brothers to finish; more often, these transitional forms of domestic industry were performed under specific individual arrangements with storekeepers and shoe manufacturers. Although the tasks were carried on for the benefit of the household, final authority and direction over them no longer belonged to the parents.

25. Homer Merriam, "My Father's History and Family," pp. 187-189.

26. Lydia Maria Child, *The Mother's Book* (Boston, 1831), p. 61. See Caroline Sloat, "The Family in the Center Village," OSV Interpretive Paper, 1980, for an account of how advice books emerged out of domestic realities.

27. Underwood, *Quabbin*, pp. 187-193 has a good brief description. Work is truly inescapable in the New England sources.

28. Mary Livermore, *The Story of My Life* (Hartford, 1899), p. 23; Lucy Larcom, *A New England Girlhood* (Boston, 1889), p. 30; Harriet Robinson, *Loom and Spindle* (Boston, 1898), pp. 22-23, 30. The themes current in this writer's childhood were taken from World War II, "Flash Gordon" and "The Lone Ranger." I would like to thank Pamela Beall for sharing her valuable insights into this topic with me.

29. Reminiscences of Susan Blunt, p. 16. Harriet Beecher Stowe saw a sharp contrast in this regard as early as the 1870s; see Stowe, *Poganuc People: Their Loves and Lives* (New York, 1878), pp. 19-21.

30. Henry Dana Ward, Travel Journal, 1823, Ward Family Papers, American Antiquarian Society.

31. See Kenneth A. Lockridge, *Literacy in Colonial New England* (New York, 1874). The emergence of the district school system in the second half of the eighteenth century greatly reduced the distance needed to travel to school; this coupled with what seems to have been a shift in attitudes about schooling for girls, created the conditions for widespread literacy.

32. Warren Burton, *The District School as it Was* (Boston, 1833 & many subsequent editions) is the classic account of schooling in the period.

33. Deborah Hood's dissertation research on school in Massachusetts in the early and middle nineteenth century has found that this pattern was widespread.

34. Hiram Munger, *Life and Religious Experience*, p. 7.

35. Homer Merriam, "My Fathers's History and Family," p. 1.

36. The pupils of the Brookfield Female Classical Seminary in 1826-27, for instance, were largely the daughters of center village merchants, artisans and professionals in central Massachusetts towns. Two of the Merriam daughters attended for a term or two. Record Book, Brookfield Female Classical Seminary, W. Brookfield, MA, 1826-28, American Antiquarian Society.

37. Massachusetts (Horace Mann), *Fourth Annual Report of the Secretary of the Board of Education,* Boston, 1841, p. 26. Also see note 38.

38. Ibid., "The Breaking Up of Schools," pp. 86-92; Greeley, *Recollections of a Busy Life,* p. 43; Reminiscences of Susan Blunt, pp. 11-12.

39. David Goodale (Sr.) School Record Book, 1810-1822, Stow, Massachusetts, OSV Research Library.

NOTES

40. See Record Books, School District No. 2, Shrewsbury, Massachusetts, 1839-50, Ward Family Papers, American Antiquarian Society, for an example of how this sort of design was discussed and adopted.

41. Alcott, *The Young Mother*, pp. 235-241; Mary Ware Howland, *The Infant School Manual* (Worcester, 1830). (Mrs. Howland, a carpenter's wife, ran an infant school in W. Brookfield Center), pp. 1-3.

42. These conclusions were derived from the analysis of the manuscript population schedules of the 1850 Federal census for Shrewsbury, Sturbridge, and West Brookfield.

43. David Stannard, *The Puritan Way of Death* (New York, 1977), ch. 2, "Death and Childhood," pp. 44-71; Ross W. Beales, Jr., "In Search of the Historical Child: Miniature Adulthood and Youth in Colonial New England," American Quarterly XXVII, (October, 1975), pp. 379-398.

44. See John S. C. Abbott, *The Mother at Home* (Boston, 1834); Child, *The Mother's Book* (1831) and Alcott, *The Young Mother* (1836) for popular examples of New England child-rearing advice in this decade. Bernard Wishy, *The Child in the Republic* (Philadelphia, 1968), provides an account of advice literature from 1830 to 1900.

45. Sloat, "Family Life in the Center Village."

46. *Journal of Zadoc Long*, pp. 80-164 *passim;* Letters, Salem Towne to Sally Towne, Oct. 19, 1822, July 25, 1824, Nov. 10, 1827, Nov. 17, 1827, June 7, 1829, Aug. 25, 1831, Towne Family Papers, OSV Research Library; *Autobiography of Lyman Beecher*, pp. 101-2, 104; Lucy Buffum Lovell, pp. 82-83.

47. Reminiscences of Susan Blunt, p. 3; "Life and Writing of Minerva Mayo by Herself," Orange, Massachusetts, 1820-22, OSV Research Library. *The Life of Asa Sheldon*, pp. 10-35, describes a violent farm household.

48. Alcott, *The Young Mother*, p. 330. Alcott's years as a rural district schoolmaster in the 1830s, frequently boarding around and visiting his pupils and their parents in their homes, and his work as a physician in a country neighborhood, gave him a wide acquaintance with how children were disciplined.

49. Abbott, *Mother at Home*, p. 30.

50. Abbott, *Mother at Home*, p. 31; Lucy Buffum Lovell, pp. 49-109. She was not a Quaker by the time of her marriage but the wife of an evangelical Baptist minister.

51. Philip M. Greven, *The Protestant Temperament* (New York, 1978) provides an extended discussion of 17th, 18th and early 19th-century child-rearing styles; Underwood, *Quabbin*, pp. 187-193, describes both "ultra-pious" and moderate styles of the 1830s. Susan I. Lesley's *Recollections of My Mother*, (the Lyman family of Northampton), Lucy Larcom's *A New England Girlhood* and Homer Merriam's, "My Father's History and Family," provide evidence on child-rearing styles. Harriet Beecher Stowe, *Oldtown Folks* (Boston, 1869), pp. 243-248, has a debate on child-raising styles between the evangelical and the traditional positions.

52. The Methodist and Episcopal churches took baptism most seriously as a sacrament admitting the child to the possibility of God's grace. Unitarians seem not to have considered it important, but to have administered it as a dedicatory rite for parents. Some Universalists rejected it altogether. For Orthodox Congregationalists, it was an essential precondition for acceptance into the church, and a symbol of parental dedication, although not itself saving.

53. Records, Congregational Church of Sturbridge, Vol. IV, 1800-1819, "Baptisms"; Vol. V, 1819-1831, "Baptisms"; Vol. VI, 1831-1895, "Baptisms to 1850."

54. See e.g. Lydia Huntley Sigourney, *Scenes in My Native Land*, pp. 102-103; Harriet Beecher Stowe, *Poganuc People*, pp. 78-79.

55. Underwood, *Quabbin*, p. 8; Sigourney, *Scenes*, p. 103; Stowe, *Poganuc People*, p. 73; and *Old Town Folks*, pp. 53-56; Calvin Wheeler Philleo, *Twice Married: A Story of Connecticut Life* (New York and London, 1855), p. 143; Elizabeth D. Ward, *Old Times in Shrewsbury, Massachusetts: Gleanings from History and Tradition* (New York, 1892), pp. 91-92.